Super Safari 2

Workbook

Herbert Puchta   **Günter Gerngross**   **Peter Lewis-Jones**

CAMBRIDGE
UNIVERSITY PRESS

Shaftesbury Road, Cambridge CB2 8EA, United Kingdom

One Liberty Plaza, 20th Floor, New York, NY 10006, USA

477 Williamstown Road, Port Melbourne, VIC 3207, Australia

314–321, 3rd Floor, Plot 3, Splendor Forum, Jasola District Centre,
New Delhi – 110025, India

103 Penang Road, #05–06/07, Visioncrest Commercial, Singapore 238467

Cambridge University Press & Assessment is a department of the University of Cambridge.

We share the University's mission to contribute to society through the pursuit of
education, learning and research at the highest international levels of excellence.

www.cambridge.org
Information on this title: www.cambridge.org/9781107482029

First published 2015

40 39 38 37 36 35 34 33 32 31

Printed in Poland by Opolgraf

A catalogue record for this publication is available from the British Library

ISBN   978-1-107-48202-9   Workbook Level 2
ISBN   978-1-107-48190-9   Student's Book with DVD-ROM Level 2
ISBN   978-1-107-48203-6   Teacher's Book Level 2
ISBN   978-1-107-48216-6   Teacher's DVD Level 2
ISBN   978-1-107-48204-3   Class Audio CDs Level 2
ISBN   978-1-107-47692-9   Flashcards Level 2
ISBN   978-1-107-48208-1   Presentation Plus DVD-ROM Level 2
ISBN   978-1-107-49662-0   Posters Level 2
ISBN   978-1-107-47732-2   Puppet

Additional resources for this publication at www.cambridge.org/supersafari/ame

Super Safari 2 Workbook

Hello!

1 Look and match. Say the names.

1  **2**  **3**  **4**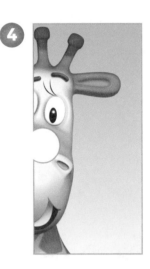

2 **Draw yourself. Say the sentences.**

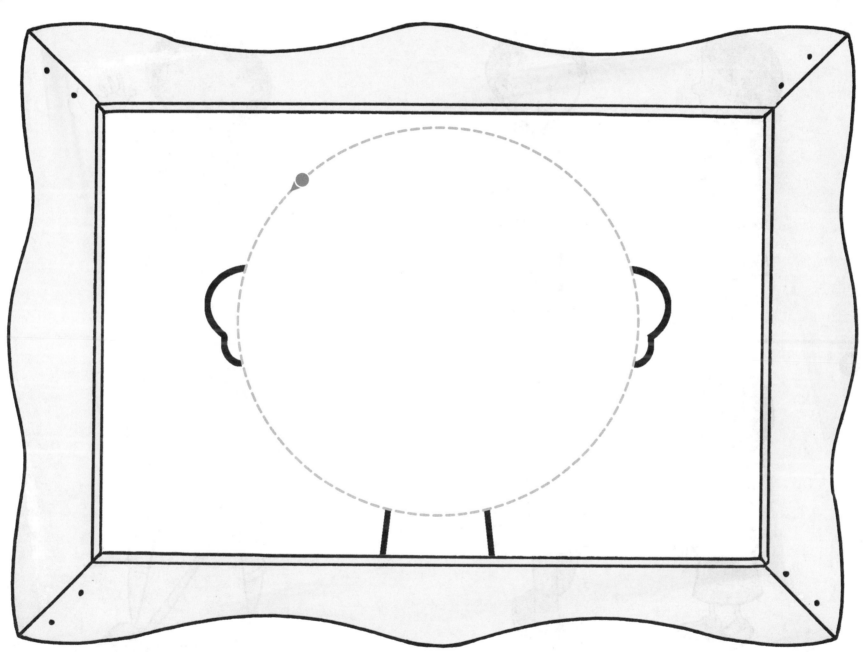

Listen and circle.

1

2

4 Say the names. Color the circles.

1

2

3

4

1 My school

1 Look, find, and circle. Say the words.

1

2

3

4

5

6

board, paper, computer, desk, crayon, pencil case

2 Listen and circle. Say the sentences.

1

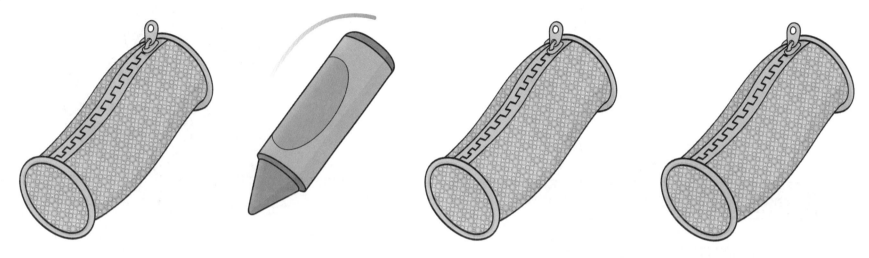

2

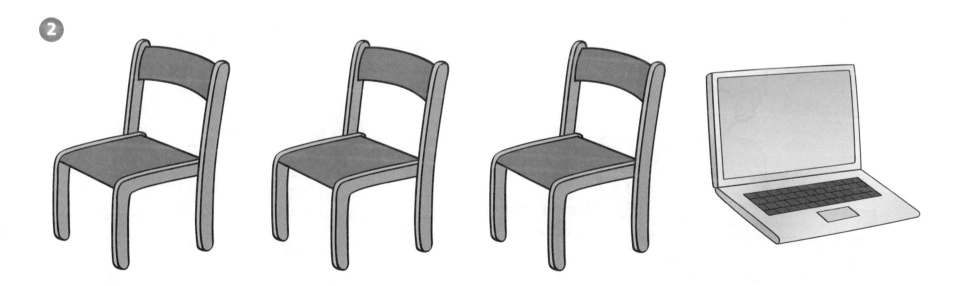

This is my (crayon). 9

3 **Listen and circle.**

1

2

 **4** Listen again. Color and complete.

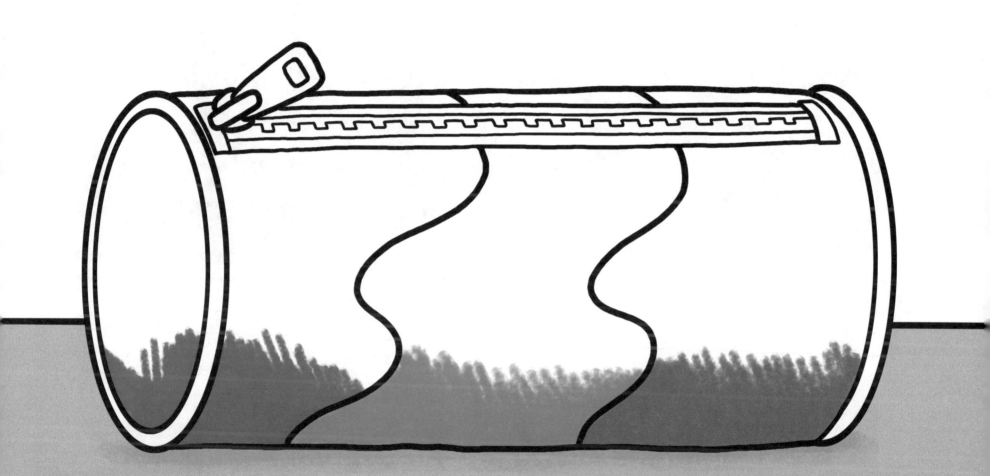

5 🔘 Listen and color the correct circles.

1

2

6 Complete the faces (☺ or ☹). Color the pictures.

7 Make a bowling game.

1

2

3

8 **Say the words. Color the circles.**

1

2

3

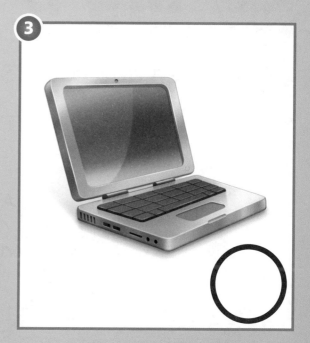

4

5

6

2 My body

1 CD1 23 **Listen and color. Say the words.**

2 CD1 25 **Listen, trace, and match. Say the sentences.**

I can (clap my hands). 17

Listen and circle.

 1

 2

4 CD1 31 **Listen again. Trace.**

5 CD1 33 **Listen and color the correct circles.**

1

2

6 Complete the faces (☺ or ☹). Color the pictures.

7 Make a self-portrait.

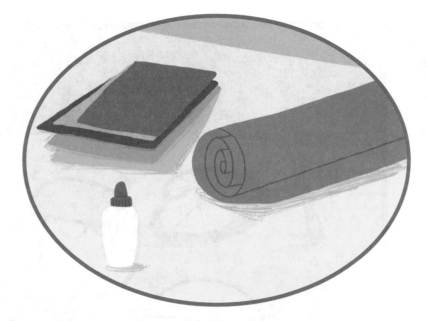

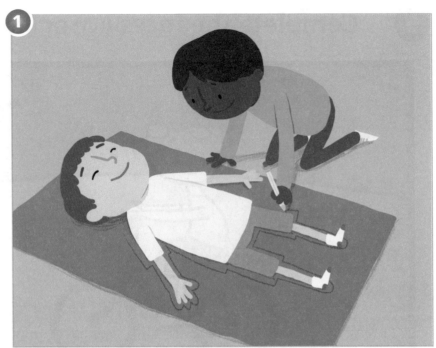

8 Say the words. Color the circles.

1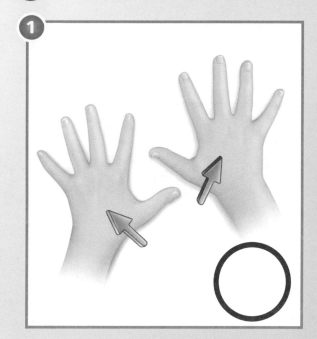

2

3

4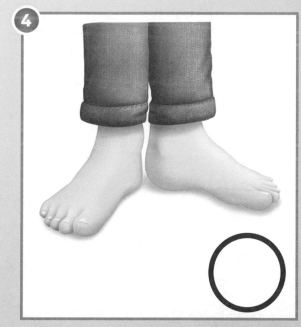

5

6

③ My room

1 Look, trace, and color. Say the words.

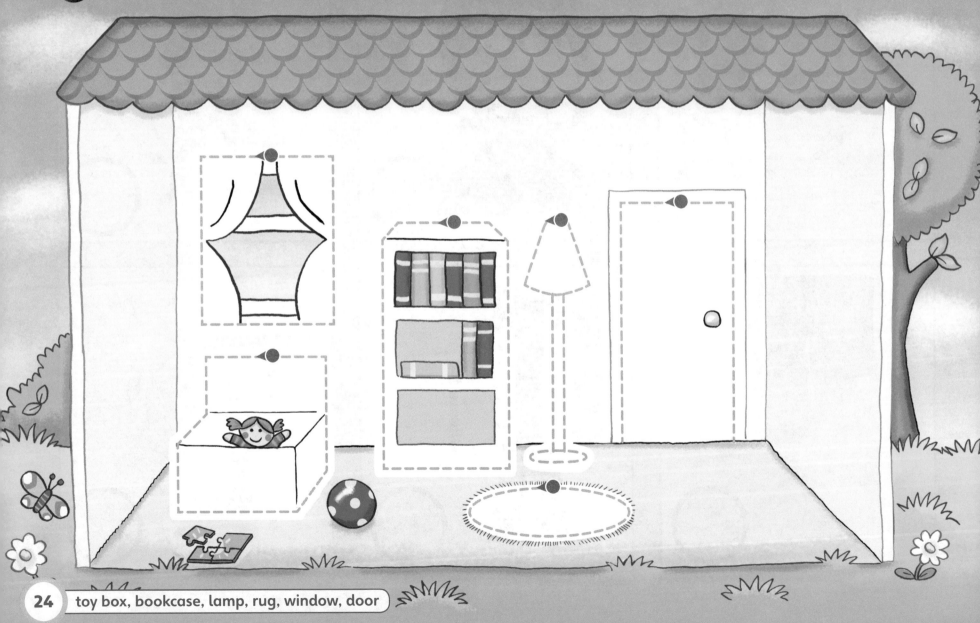

toy box, bookcase, lamp, rug, window, door

2 CD1 38 **Listen and color. Say the sentences.**

1
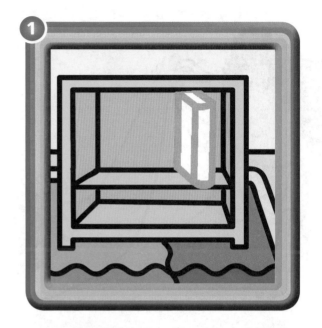

2
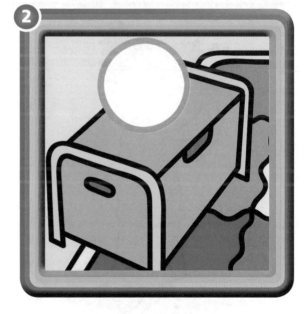

3
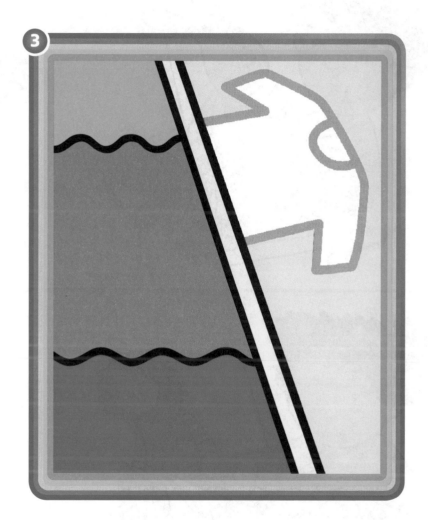

Where's my (book)? It's in / on / under the (bookcase). **25**

Listen and circle.

1

2

4 Listen again. Draw your room.

Listen and color the correct circles.

1

2

6 Complete the faces (☺ or ☹). Color the pictures.

7 **Make a poster of your room.**

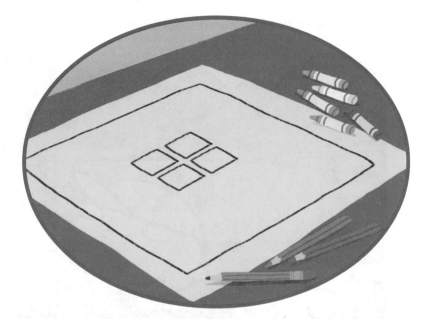

8 **Say the words. Color the circles.**

1

2

3
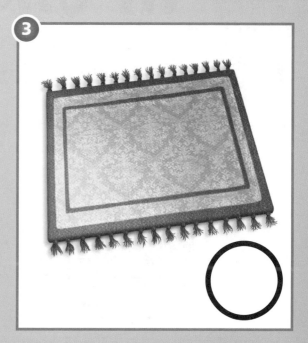

4

5

6

Listen and circle. Say the animals.

1

2

rhino, tiger, elephant, snake, spider, crocodile

2 CD1 52 Listen and connect the dots. Say the sentences.

Is it a (crocodile)? Yes, it is. / No, it isn't.   33

Listen and circle.

1

  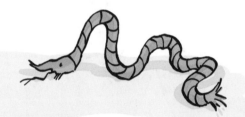

2

4 CD1 58 Listen again. Follow and trace.

Listen and color the correct circles.

1

2

6 Complete the faces (☺ or ☹). Color the pictures.

7 Make a jungle collage.

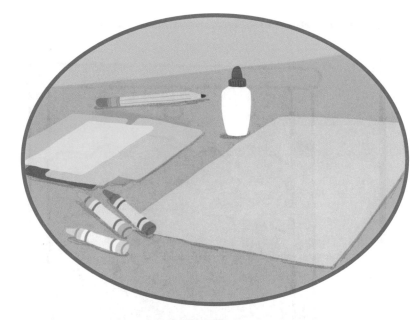

8 Say the animals. Color the circles.

1
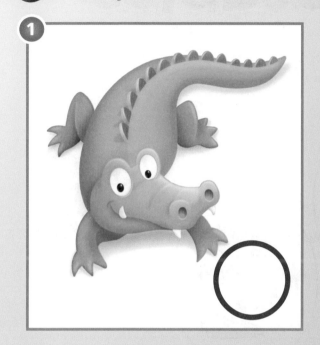

2

3

4

5

6

5 Fruits and vegetables

Listen and match. Count and say the food.

potatoes, pineapple, carrots, tomatoes, watermelon, bananas

2 Draw lines to the food you  and .

Listen and circle.

1

2

4 Listen again. Match and say the words.

1

2

5 **Listen and color the correct circles.**

1

2

6 Complete the faces (☺ or ☹). Color the pictures.

7 Make a fruit and vegetable print poster.

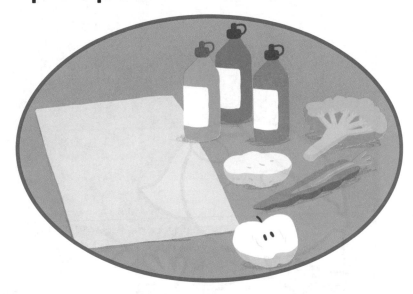

8 **Say the words. Color the circles.**

1

2

3

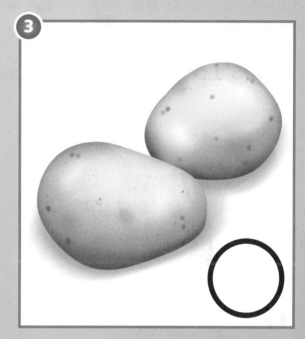

4

5

6

6 My town

1 Look and circle. Say the places.

1

2

3

bus stop, park, school, toy store, supermarket, zoo

2 Look and follow the paths. Trace and say the sentences.

1

2

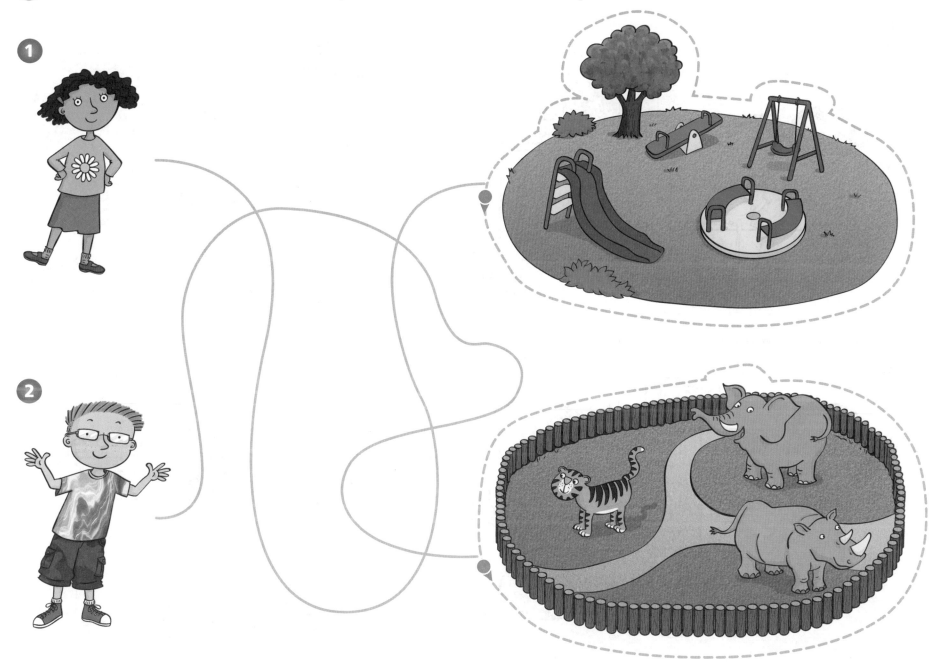

3 **Listen and circle.**

1

2

4 **Listen again. Draw your town.**

Listen and color the correct circles.

1

2

Complete the faces (☺ or ☹). Color the pictures.

7 **Make a recycling poster.**

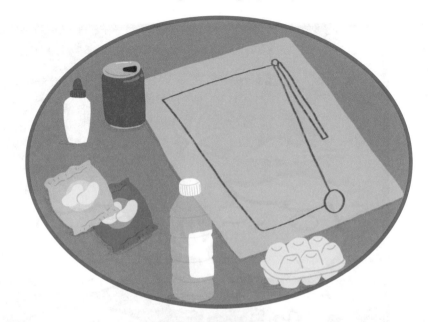

8 Say the places. Color the circles.

1

2

3

4

5

6

7 Jobs

1 Look and circle the one that doesn't belong. Say the jobs.

1

2

3

farmer, police officer, builder, doctor, firefighter, teacher

2 CD2 25 Listen, trace, and match. Say the sentences.

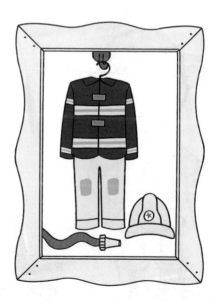

My (mom)'s a (firefighter). 57

Listen and circle.

1

2

4 CD2 31 **Listen again. Trace and color.**

6 Complete the faces (☺ or ☹). Color the pictures.

7 Make a fire engine costume.

1

2

3

8 Say the jobs. Color the circles.

1

2

3

4

5

6

8 The weather

1 **Look and match. Say the weather.**

rainy, windy, cold, snowy, hot, sunny

2 **Look and trace. Say the sentences.**

1

2

4 CD2 43 Listen again. Trace and match.

1

2

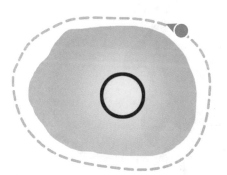

5 Listen and color the correct circles.

1

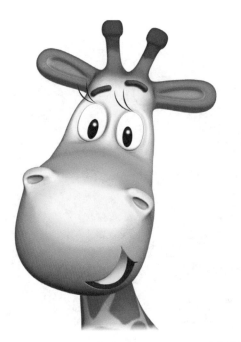

2

6 Complete the faces (☺ or ☹). Color the pictures.

7 **Make a weather dial.**

1

2

3

8 Say the weather. Color the circles.

1

2

3

4

5

6

⑨ In the country

1 What's next? Match and say the words.

1

2

3

tree, leaves, frog, grass, flower, bee

2 CD2 50 **Listen and trace. Say the sentences.**

1

2

The (bee) is / isn't (small). It's (big). **73**

Listen and circle.

1

2

4 CD2 56 **Listen again. Trace and color.**

5 **Listen and color the correct circles.**

1

2

6 **Complete the faces (☺ or ☹). Color the pictures.**

7 Make a pond collage.

8 Say the words. Color the circles.

1

2

3

4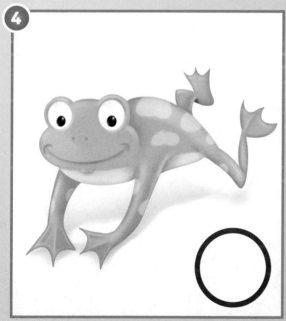

5

6

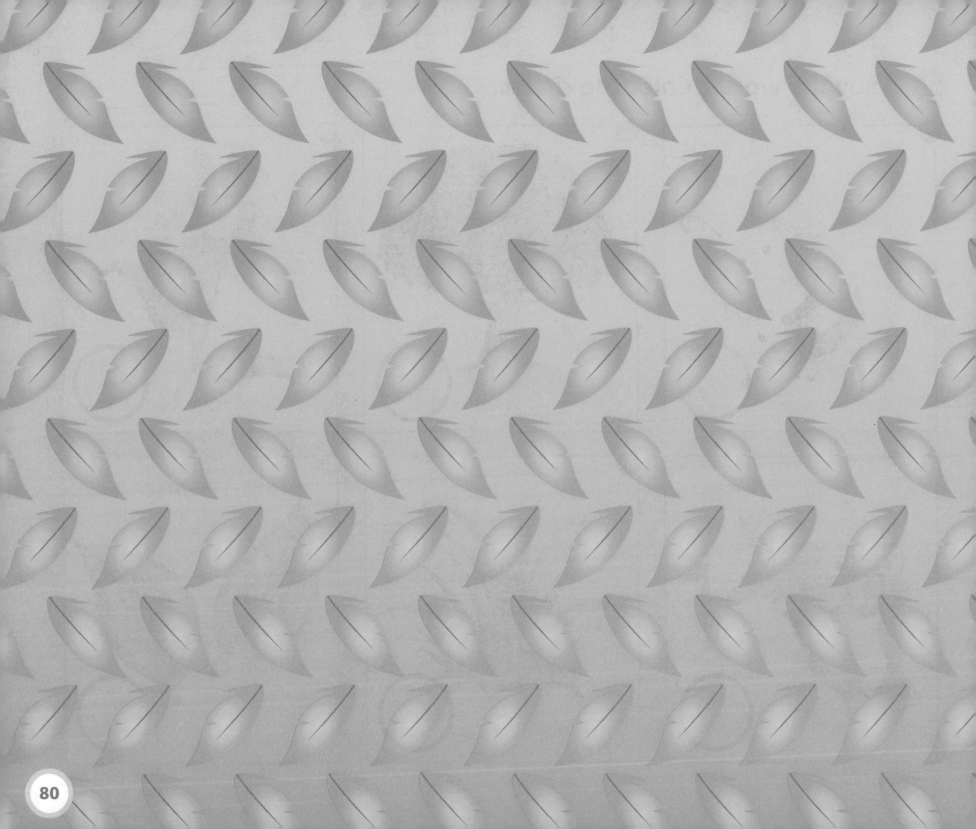

dad

cat

pin

sit

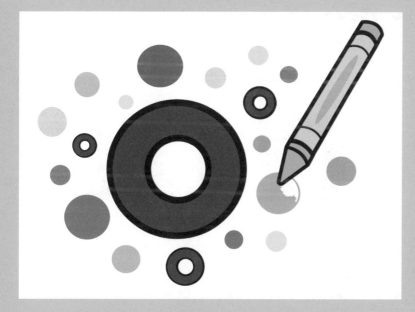

pen

bed

pot

dot

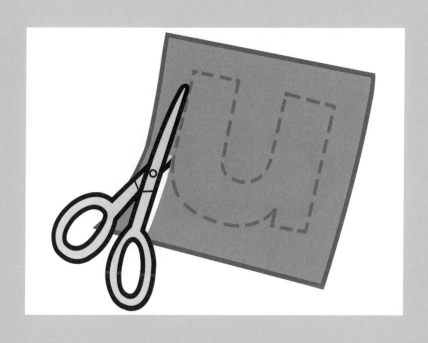

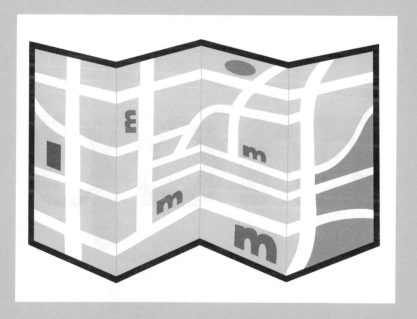

bus

cut

map

mom

job

jam

lamp

log

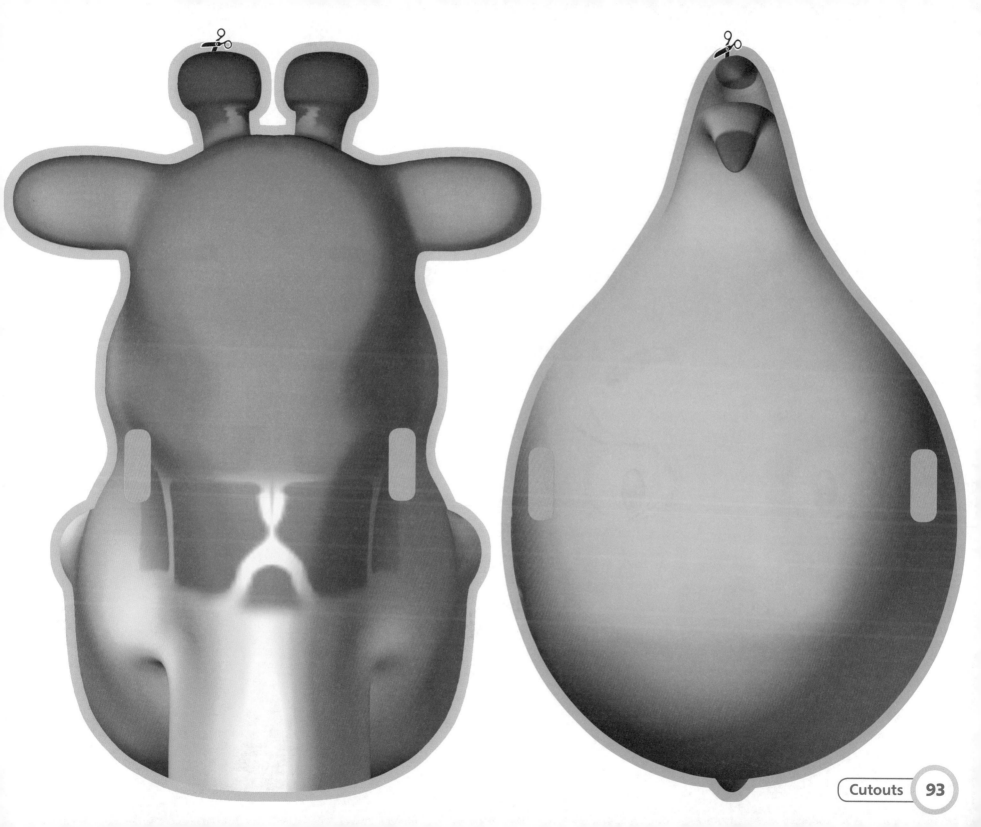

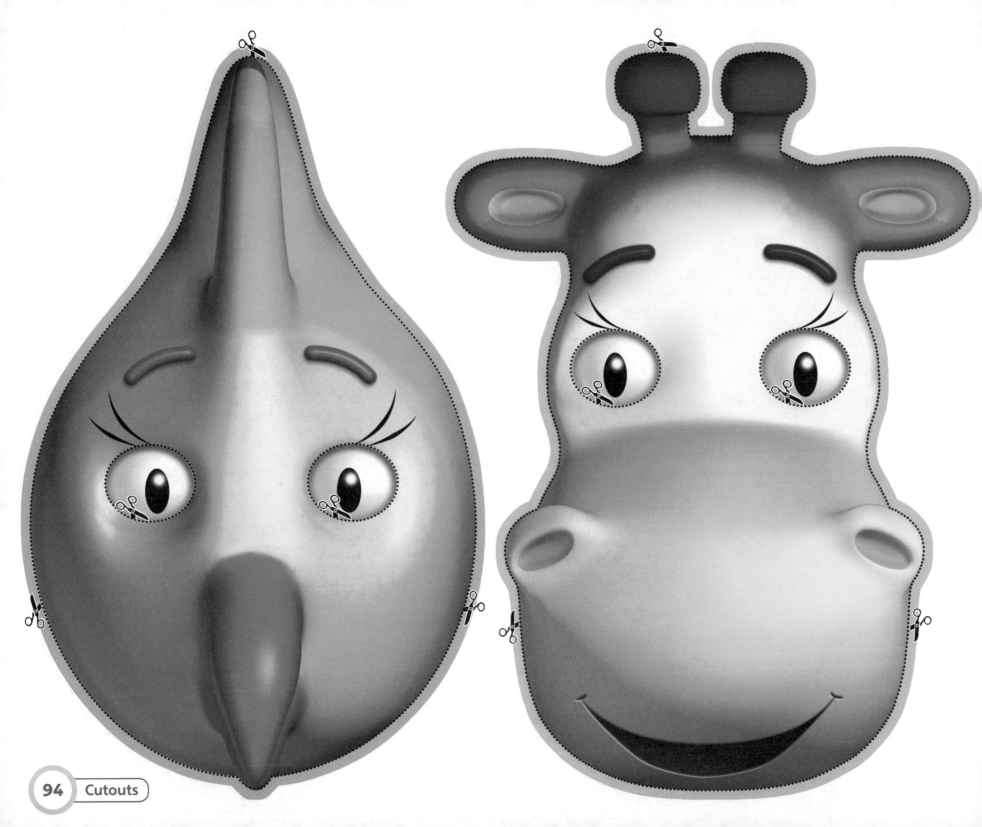

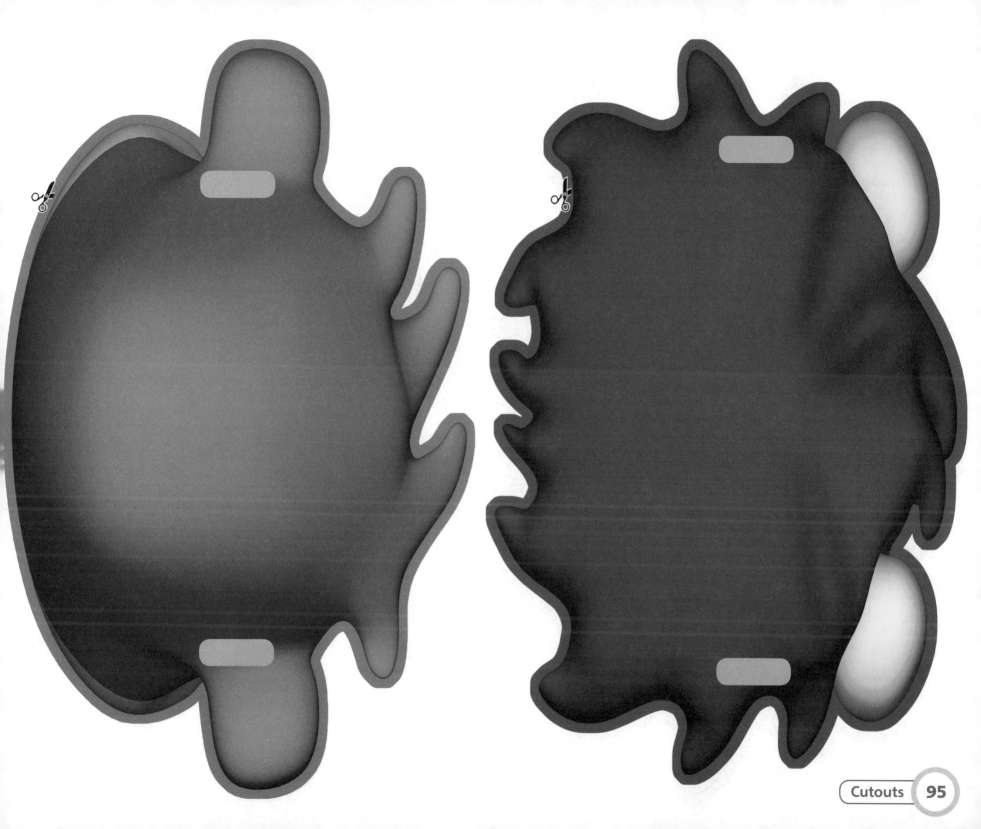

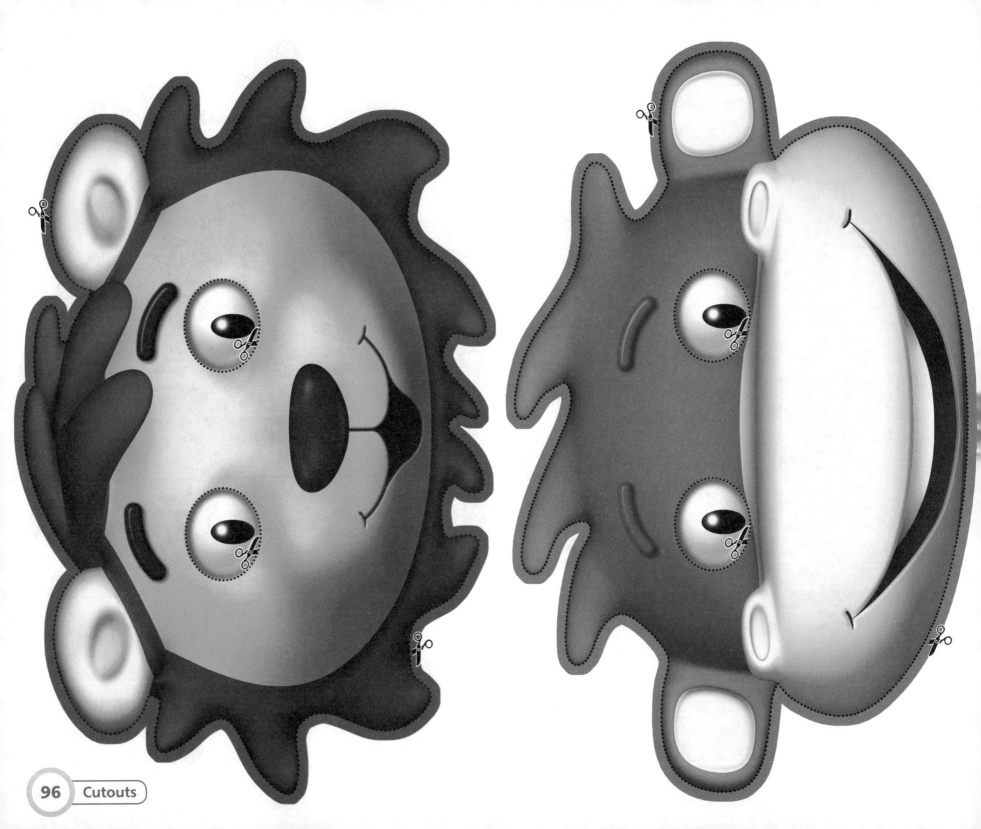